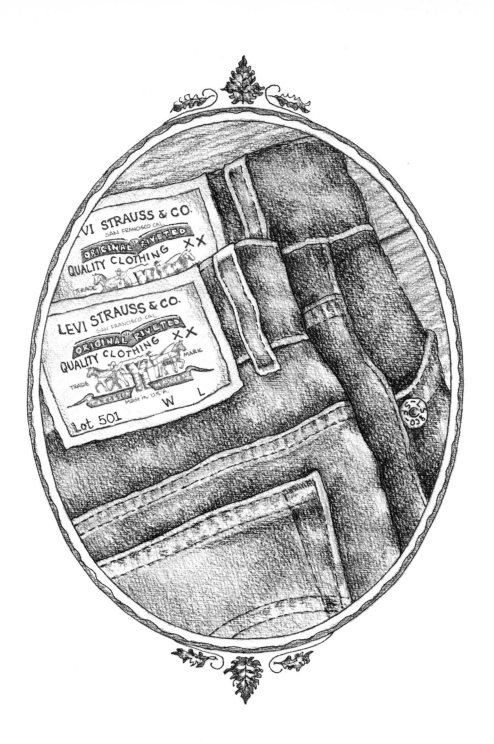

Mr. Blue Jeans

A Story about Levi Strauss

by Maryann N. Weidt
illustrations by Lydia M. Anderson

A Carolrhoda Creative Minds Book

Carolrhoda Books, Inc./Minneapolis

To Andy — Happy Birthday!

Library of Congress Cataloging-in-Publication Data

Weidt, Maryann N.
   Mr. Blue Jeans : a story about Levi Strauss / by Maryann N. Weidt;
illustrations by Lydia M. Anderson.
      p.   cm. — (A Carolrhoda creative minds book)
   Includes bibliographical references.
   Summary: Traces the life of the immigrant Jewish peddler who
went on to found Levi Strauss & Co., the world's first and largest
manufacturer of denim jeans.
   ISBN 0-87614-421-0
   1. Strauss, Levi, 1829-1902 — Juvenile literature. 2. Businessmen —
United States — Biography — Juvenile literature. 3. Levi Strauss and
Company — History — Juvenile literature. 4. Clothing trade — United
States — History — Juvenile literature. 5. Jeans (Clothing) — History —
Juvenile literature. 1. Strauss, Levi, 1829-1902. 2. Businessmen.
3. Levi Strauss and Company — History. 4. Clothing trade.
I. Anderson, Lydia M., ill. II. Title. III. Title: Mr. Blue Jeans.
IV. Series
HD9940.U4S799   1990
338.7'687'092 — dc20
[B]
[92]   89-71159
                                                           CIP

Manufactured in the United States of America

1 2 3 4 5 6 7 8 9 10 99 98 97 96 95 94 93 92 91 90

Table of Contents

6

①

Buttenheim

Gold in the steets. Gold instead of mud. What a relief that would be! Löb Strauss (who would later be called Levi) looked down at his muddy boots and the soggy streets of Buttenheim. This tiny village sat at the foot of the Bavarian Alps, near the German/Austrian border. Every spring when the snow melted, water ran down the mountainsides and turned the streets to mud.

Löb hauled his peddler's pack up one mucky, narrow lane and down another. High above him, tiny pink and yellow blossoms cascaded from the window boxes of old stone and timber houses. Though hundreds of years old, the murals on many homes looked wet and freshly painted.

"Dry goods for sale," Löb called. An elderly man and his wife waved to him from their doorway, and Löb walked over.

"What have you brought us today?" the man asked. Löb pulled the heavy pack off his shoulders and laid it over his knee. Careful not to let anything fall into the mud, Löb showed them his assortment of buttons and lace, shovels and hoes, spoons and cooking pots. The woman chose a bit of lace for a woolen dress she was sewing. The man picked out a hoe. Löb thanked them and trudged on.

Löb was born in Buttenheim in 1829. His father, Hirsch Strauss, had also grown up in this centuries-old village. Hirsch had kept his family warm and fed by selling dry goods. Since his father's death two years earlier, Löb, his mother, and his sisters had struggled to survive. So Löb had taken up his father's trade to help out.

As he lugged his heavy pack from door to door, eighteen-year-old Löb heard endless stories about people who had moved to America. It was said that many who had gone there as beggars were now wealthy. "The streets are lined with gold," people told one another. "The gold is there for the taking."

Löb's stepbrothers, Louis and Jonas, had gone to New York after their father's death. They had written back to Löb that in America, even Jewish men could vote. Now that was something!

In Bavaria Jews could not vote. No one could. But with each new royal Bavarian ruler came new rules against the Jews. This had been going on for hundreds of years. The Bavarian government had even gone so far as to say how many Jewish couples could be married in a year. With fewer marriages, there would be fewer Jewish babies.

Löb knew that if he stayed in Buttenheim, the government would tell him what he could do for a living and where he must live. Already Löb and his family could not live on most streets in the village. They had to make their home on what was known as Jew Street. In addition the Strausses had to pay special taxes on their home and business because they were Jewish.

In America Löb could be what he wanted to be and live where he wanted to live. As for taxes, he wasn't sure. But with all the gold in the streets, taxes couldn't be that much of a problem.

As many as ten thousand Jews had already left Bavaria for the new land. In the nearby village of Hagenbach, twelve young men planned to leave the country just after the spring feast of Passover. In Buttenheim many Jews had left as well. Löb wanted to follow their example.

All of April and May, when Löb was not slogging through the mud, he was talking to his mother and his sisters, Vögela and Maila, about going to New York. Letters continued to arrive from Louis and Jonas telling of the wonders of the new land. The brothers wrote that they were considered "greenhorns" by those who had come before them. Yet they were able to make a good living by working hard and being careful with their money. They could not complain.

By June of 1847, Rebecca Strauss, Löb's mother, was convinced. She asked the courts in Bamberg for the documents she and her family needed to leave the country. Her petition was granted. The Strausses prepared to leave their home.

The family packed very little since they could not bring much on the ship. They had heard many stories about life at sea, so they knew that they should bring their own food. The food aboard the ship would not be prepared in the proper Jewish manner. Besides kosher food, Löb's mother packed bedding, the family's brass candlesticks, and their samovar, which was used to heat water for tea. Rebecca told their friends and neighbors to take whatever they wanted of the things the Strausses would leave behind.

The port city of Bremen was crowded with people carrying bundles, bags, and trunks. After a few days in the harbor, the ship set sail. Löb was thankful, despite the fishy smell, that his mother had packed plenty of herring, as well as black bread and tea. Day after day, the other passengers had to eat beans and pork, pork and beans. Still, when the ship began to roll, it did not matter much to Löb what he had eaten. Most of it did not stay in his stomach anyway.

Which was worse, Löb wondered, to be seasick below deck in the meager, cramped quarters or to be on deck with the constant threat of being washed overboard?

The compartment below deck was so small that a normal-sized person could not stand up straight. Plus, it was damp and dirty. How could it be otherwise with three hundred people packed into a space the size of a small barn? Privacy was nearly impossible, and the only water for washing was salt water.

The passengers lived so close to one another that when one was seasick, it was hard not to be sick on top of another traveler. A board and a blanket served as a bed, with barely enough space for sleeping. There was certainly no room for anyone to unpack or hang up any clothes.

Yet, as bad as it was, life at sea did have some variation. Over the course of the trip, three babies were born and one old man died. Many days someone would pick up a fiddle or a flute, and others would join in song. On occasion a few people would even try to dance on deck.

After forty-two days at sea, land was spotted. The ship pulled steadily into New York harbor. Sailing vessels from all over the world packed the bay. Löb strained forward at the railing to see if his brothers were waiting for them. He could not find them in the swarm of people on the docks. Behind the crowds, four- and five-story buildings rose higher than any houses in Buttenheim. In the far distance, cows grazed in the fields outside the city.

It seemed like hours before the enormous ship was tied to the dock. Finally the plank went down, and the immigrants started to go ashore. As they left the ship, the captain checked each person's name. It was his duty to send this final list of passengers to the United States government.

Löb stood in line with his family and the other passengers. When it was his turn, he stepped forward and told the captain his name. The man checked his list and barked something back to him that sounded like Levi.

Löb was confused. Was he to be called Levi from now on?

Löb remembered stories about people getting new American names. The captain had also called his sisters, Maila and Vögela, by new names—Mary and Fanny.

Löb considered the sound of it—Levi. He wanted to make the United States his new home. So he decided that if they wanted to call him Levi, then Levi it would be.

Levi followed his family ashore. They walked away from the crowded docks to a street filled with people bustling in all directions. Vendors with pushcarts were selling every item imaginable. Each seller shouted louder than the last. "Apples!" "Flowers!" "Boots!"

Levi didn't know what the words meant. It was as if he were being washed overboard in a sea of words. Then from a distance came the sound of his Bavarian name, "Löb!" Bewildered, he looked around. He saw his brothers, Louis and Jonas, running toward him. Words poured from them, German and Hebrew words that Levi understood.

Louis and Jonas embraced the little group with

delight, talking excitedly. They had found a place for the women to stay. Relatives living on the lower East Side of New York would be happy to have them, at least for a while. Levi could live with his brothers in a peddlers' rooming house.

As Louis and Jonas showed the family the city sights, Levi noticed that some of the streets were lined with cobblestones, not gold. At least, Levi thought, they're not filled with mud.

The Peddler

At the peddlers' rooming house, Levi and his brothers had one good meal a day, a bed, and a chance to wash up. Rent was three dollars a month for each.

Levi had little money, which was not surprising. Most immigrants came to America with about twenty dollars in their pockets. Luckily for Levi, his brothers had made some money as pack peddlers and were willing to help get him started. Louis and Jonas supplied Levi with his first goods.

Each day Levi shouldered his fifty-pound pack and tramped the streets of New York City, trying to sell needles and pins, ribbons and cloth. At first Levi did not even know the right English words for his wares. He would simply open his pack and say, "Goods for sale." People passing by would stop and pick something out. Then they would press a penny, or a nickle, or maybe even a dime into his hand.

"Thank you," he would say. He knew that much.

It didn't take Levi long, though, to make the transition from his German sprinkled with Hebrew to the language of his new home. He could soon count money, make change, and read the peddler maps. He even became used to the sound of his new name—Levi Strauss.

By the end of each day, Levi's back hurt and his feet were sore. But in very little time, he had paid back his brothers and had begun to make money of his own.

New York City was crowded with merchants and peddlers. Levi knew that he would get more sales where there were fewer people selling. So within a year, he ventured beyond New York City to towns as far away as Pelham, New York.

As a country peddler, Levi had to walk farther and carry a heavier load. Country peddlers traveled with two packs—a one-hundred-pound pack on their backs and an eighty-pound pack strapped on their chests. They had to haul a greater variety of goods because they never knew what the farmers would need. And since the peddlers wouldn't be returning to the city every evening, they had to pack enough merchandise for a week of selling.

As Levi walked, he toted many of the same things he had sold in the city: pins, ribbons, and thread. But he also lugged along pots, pans, shovels, and hoes as he once had in Buttenheim.

Strangely enough the more Levi sold, the heavier his load became. Many times he was paid not in paper or coins, but in sacks of grain or in tins of honey or molasses.

Peddling in the country was not easy. In winter Levi walked through blowing snow so thick he could not see the road on either side. In spring he faced the danger of losing what was left of his shoes in ankle-deep mud. Most of the time, he did not know where he would sleep at night. Sometimes a kind farmer would invite him to spend the night in a barn or stable. In less fortunate times, he would have to bed down somewhere in the woods or alongside the road.

There were some advantages, though, to country peddling. Young rowdies did not often throw stones at him or snowballs with pieces of coal inside as they did in the city. Nor did Levi have to worry about being attacked in a dark alleyway and having his goods and money stolen. Instead, people usually welcomed him because he brought news of neighboring villages.

As Levi trudged along the dusty trails and swampy paths of New York State, he thought about what the rest of America might look like. Soon he was given a chance to find out.

In 1848 Levi learned that a relative had settled in Louisville, Kentucky. Without delay Levi said good-bye to his family and set off on foot to visit his newly discovered kin. It took Levi awhile, but he eventually arrived in the wild frontier state of Kentucky. He stayed for five years, peddling his wares in the Appalachian foothills.

The people of Kentucky were friendly and treated Levi with respect. In return for their kindness, Levi would give the housewives and their daughters two-for-a-penny spools of thread or a packet of pins.

Sometimes Levi was invited to share a meal with a family. He would gratefully accept, even if the food was not always kosher.

Every night before settling under a tree or in someone's barn, Levi washed out his only pair of socks. It was a tradition that had been handed down through generations of pack peddlers. As Levi hung the socks to dry, he hoped they would not be soggy in the morning. Otherwise he would have to wear them wet and squishing in his boots.

21

Still, it would not be the first time since he came to America that he would have wet feet.

From 1848 to 1852, while Levi was peddling in Kentucky, his brothers were operating a dry goods store in New York City. A directory of New York City in 1848 listed Jonas Strauss as the owner of a store at 203½ Division Street. By 1851 the brothers had moved to a larger store at 165 Houston Street. They wrote to Levi, asking him to join them.

Despite the hardships of peddling, though, Levi was not interested in going back to New York. There was another city Levi was interested in— San Francisco.

The news of the gold rush in California had traveled east. Levi knew of people who had gone to find gold. Many had returned disappointed. Some had never been heard from again. But plenty had struck it rich.

Levi's sister Fanny had written to him from San Francisco. She and her husband, David Stern, had just recently arrived there. The young newlyweds had traveled to San Francisco to start a business in that gold-struck boomtown, and they wanted Levi to join them.

Levi knew it was a risk to go to California, but coming to the United States had also been a risk.

Take a chance, Levi thought to himself. Otherwise you will never know what you have missed.
In San Francisco, you might finally see those
legendary streets of gold.

Around the Horn

In late 1852 or early 1853, Levi journeyed back to New York City to bid farewell to his family. After a short visit, he trundled his peddler's pack to the docks of New York Harbor. His pack was loaded with bolts of canvas cloth to be used for miners' tents, and other items Levi thought the citizens of San Francisco might need.

On this voyage, Levi was on his own. But well he should be, he thought. He was twenty-four years old and no longer a greenhorn.

Levi's brothers came to see him off. They reminded him of the difficulties of being a peddler and urged him to stay with them and work in the store. But Levi's mind was set. He was bound for the West Coast, where he could sell his goods to the gold seekers of California.

Amid hymn singing and handkerchief waving, Levi boarded the sleek clipper ship. A bitter winter wind whipped his face and hands as he waved to his family on shore.

Would he ever see them again? he wondered. Perhaps he would not survive the voyage around South America's Cape Horn. Maybe the ship, solid as it seemed, would not hold together. He had heard stories of others who had set out for the California gold fields and never arrived. Many people had died of cholera, malaria, or some other tropical disease.

At this time, though, going by sea was the surest way to get from the East Coast of the United States to the new states on the West Coast. There were no railroad lines that crossed the Mississippi River or the Rocky Mountains. And to go by the Oregon-California Trail meant a walk of a thousand miles over the plains and another thousand miles over rougher territory.

NORTH AMERICA

San Francisco

New York

Panama

Routes Westward

SOUTH AMERICA

Cape Horn

N
W E
S

1853

Yet the sea route was neither quick nor easy. Since there was no canal cutting through Central America, ships had to travel around the southern-most tip of South America and up the western coasts of the Americas to reach California.

The only other choice was to travel south by ship to Panama and then walk across the country to catch a ship on the other side. This idea did not appeal to Levi.

Levi went below deck to take a look at what would be his home for the next four months. He had paid $250 for a bunk in a large room with fifty identical cots. The cots seemed only slightly wider than the boards that had served as beds on the journey from Bavaria. Levi hoped he would not be seasick as he had been then. But it did little good to hope. His stomach would make the final decision for him.

Levi was not alone in his quest to see mountain streams sparkling with gold dust. One hundred and fifty others—mostly men—joined him on the ship. There were doctors and merchants, farmers and sea captains, a clergyman, a geologist, and other peddlers like himself. In the four years since prospectors had started staking their claims, word had traveled back to New York that those who had found gold needed trinkets to buy with their money. Levi was not the only one who wanted to take advantage of this business opportunity.

Days aboard ship passed quickly. Despite the surly appearance of some of his shipmates, Levi found they were not a bad lot. Some looked—and smelled—like they had never seen a wash basin. Others were so loud they could be heard from one end of the ship to the other. Several used their fists better than they used their mouths. But most just enjoyed sitting and talking the time away or reading. One or two had brought games to pass the time: backgammon, chess, and checkers. Levi was frequently invited to play.

Before long, Levi had devoured the food his mother had packed for him. Then he was faced with the grim prospect of eating the ship's rations. A standard meal was a concoction called lob-scouse. It was made from potatoes, salt beef or pork, and hard bread. Although it oozed with grease, Levi ate it. It could be worse, he thought. Stories went around that on one ship, passengers had been served wormy cereal, weevil-infested flour, and beans that had two bugs for every bean. So as long as Levi's stomach did not complain, he would eat lobscouse.

At times the sea itself provided some variety in the menu. According to one story, the captain caught a small shark and had it prepared for the evening meal. When one of the passengers complained, the captain replied, "You may as well eat him, for if you should happen to fall overboard, he would not hesitate to eat you."

Occasionally the ship stopped so water barrels could be refilled. Passengers had the chance at these stops to sample some of the unusual fruits of South America—pineapples, quinces, mangoes, and papaya. Levi had never tasted such exotic treats. He bought as many mangoes and papayas as he could carry back to the ship, thinking he would surprise his sister Fanny and her husband with them once he arrived in San Francisco. But to his disappointment, the fruit turned brown and rotted in the heat.

Rounding Cape Horn was the most difficult part of the voyage. The sea tossed the clipper ship back and forth. The waters crashed over the ship's sides, soaking anyone on deck. Passengers and crew alike had to hang on to the rigging ropes or be swept overboard. The sailors fought rain, wind, and waves to navigate around the cape's jagged rocks.

Fortunately it was summer in the southern hemisphere, and the ship did not run into snow or hail. Levi was glad he had chosen to make the trip in January rather than July.

As it had been on the way to the Cape Horn, the heat near the equator was more severe than any Levi had experienced as a peddler. It was too hot to stay below deck, where no air moved. Up above, a slight breeze stirred, but the sun beat down mercilessly. There was nowhere to hide. Levi looked down at the cool ocean and wished he could jump in and swim with the fish.

One morning Levi awoke to a chilly wind. He had gone to bed in his underwear, and now he pulled the thin blanket up to his neck. As he lay there, his sun-burned body shivering, he heard the words he had been waiting for, "Land ho!"

Levi jumped up, pulled on his woolen trousers and unfolded one of his good shirts. He wanted to make a favorable impression on his sister's new husband, the businessman.

Tough Trousers

Levi squeezed in along the ship's rail to look at the town he would now call home. The rugged cliffs and hills of lush grasses had a golden glow in the dawn. Stately cedar trees dotted the rough landscape, and the masts of abandoned ships lined the bay.

The ship pulled up to the port's Long Wharf, which jutted out into the water. Men in small boats rowed out to meet the ship and clambered on board. They came to see what the passengers had to sell. Levi brought out a bolt of canvas and began cutting off great lengths of it. Gold nuggets were placed in his hand. He fetched other items from his pack. The eager miners paid him two dollars in gold for needles that he had sold for twenty-five cents in Kentucky. Levi had not thought finding gold would be this easy.

By the time the ship had docked, Levi had sold most of his goods. He came ashore and waited for Fanny and David. Up and down the wharf, prospectors were stopping people and asking to buy Cuban cigars, tobacco in small packages, or seeds in air-tight tins. One new arrival made a handsome profit selling the shoes right off his feet. Levi watched as the man stood in his stockings, telling everyone this wonderous tale. These Californians will buy anything and everything, Levi thought. It should be no trouble at all selling things here.

In a short while, a tall, dark-haired man walked up to Levi with his arm outstretched. Levi knew this must be Fanny's husband, David Stern. Fanny had a meal waiting for them, his brother-in-law told him, and the two men started to walk uphill toward the house.

SAN FRANCISCO ÷ CALIFORNIA 1853

Levi looked about, amazed. Though it was morning, piano music and rowdy songs rang out from gambling houses. Wagons bounced over deep ruts in unpaved streets, and wooden planks served as sidewalks. Few corners had street lamps.

Levi also noticed that there were nearly as many tents as there were timber shanties. Many of the buildings were made of canvas sails that had been stripped from abandoned ships. San Francisco looked wild and young. This will be an exciting place for a businessman, Levi thought, especially for one selling cloth!

After dinner that evening, Levi told his sister and her husband tales of his shipboard adventures. Fanny and David took turns telling stories of San Francisco and the mining camps. It is a rough town, they explained regretfully. Murders and holdups occur daily.

Early the next morning, Levi walked with David Stern to his dry goods store at the foot of Sacramento Street. David told Levi more about San Francisco on the way. As near as David could estimate, there were 4 saw mills, 5 theaters, 23 wharves, 28 breweries, 117 dry goods stores, and 399 saloons. "All this," David concluded, "in a town of seventy-eight thousand people."

Imagine that, thought Levi, there are more saloons than dry goods stores.

David Stern had been a pack peddler in St. Louis before coming to San Francisco in 1851. His dry goods establishment was young, and it was fortunate for him that Levi arrived when he did. David had had difficulty finding clerks since most young men—and even old men—were on their way to the mines. Within weeks of his arrival, Levi was an important part of the business as well as the Stern household.

Levi Strauss and David Stern did well in the store on Sacramento Street. They sold pants and shirts as well as blankets, tin plates, cups, and other household items. Some goods came to them by river steamer and stage coach. But most of the merchandise traveled from New York on clipper ships—especially the heavy bolts of fabric supplied by Levi's brothers.

When a ship was due to arrive, Levi and David slept in the shop on blankets they had pulled off the shelves. Sometimes they hired a young boy to stand atop the city's tallest building or highest hill to watch for the approaching vessel. When the ship was sighted, Levi and David quickly marked down the prices on the items they had left in stock. They wanted to empty their shelves of old goods as quickly as possible to make room for new merchandise. Then before the ship had even docked, Levi would be standing at the wharf, ready for the ship's auction to begin. He would bid for merchandise while David continued to mark down the leftover goods.

By 1856 the store on Sacramento Street was too small for the growing business. Levi was now a partner, and the two men moved their operation to a larger store a few doors up—at 117 Sacramento Street. Levi and David also changed the way they did business. They became wholesalers as well as retailers, selling merchandise to other stores in addition to individual customers.

To drum up sales from shops in the mining camps, Levi once again became a peddler. This time he bought himself a wagon for fifty dollars and a mule for twenty-five dollars. He packed up hats, shirts, and canvas in large trunks and loaded these onto his wagon. Then he and his wagon boarded a sidewheel steamer to travel up the Sacramento River to California's bustling new capital. From Sacramento he followed wagon paths to gold towns like El Dorado and Placerville that had sprung up along the river.

One sunny day, Levi was enjoying his lunch on the banks of the Sacramento River. A miner came by and asked Levi what he had for sale. Levi pulled a bolt of canvas out of his wagon and suggested that the prospector take a new tent to the diggings. The miner said that he didn't need a tent but could use some good, sturdy pants. Levi thought for a moment and then looked for a piece of string. Using a length of cording, he took the man's measurements. He told the fellow he would have a pair of long-wearing pants by sundown.

Now Levi had to find a tailor to make the pants. It was not as easy as he thought it would be. Many of the tailors had gone to seek their fortunes in the mines. Finally Levi found one in a nearby town who had not been caught up by gold fever. Levi asked the man to make a pair of canvas pants in the miner's size and to sew the rest of the fabric into various other sizes.

That evening Levi found the prospector near the place he had left him and presented him with the pants. The miner could not believe his good luck. He grabbed the pants and pulled them on right over his ragged old trousers. The pants felt like they would last, and the miner reckoned that the pockets were big enough for his gold samples.

He cheerfully paid Levi six dollars in gold dust.

Before long the miner had spread the word in the gold camps along the river about "those pants of Levi's." Soon Levi had sold all the pants he had ordered from the tailor.

Levi wrote to his brothers in New York and ordered additional canvas for more pants. The fabric they shipped, however, was not canvas but a heavy cotton material called denim. Made in the French town of Nimes, the cloth was named denim (for *de Nimes*) by the Americans. Pants made of this denim were popular with Genoese sailors and came to be nicknamed jeans after the Italian city of Genoa.

Within a few years, miners were not the only ones wearing Levi's pants. Overland traders carried the news of these new trousers to the Southwest and especially to Texas. Cowboys liked them because they lasted longer and were more comfortable to wear in the saddle than other pants. The men who came West to work on the railroad found that Levi's pants could withstand the long days they put in. Farmers wore them as well. They called the pants waist-high overalls, a name Levi himself preferred.

No one knows for sure if the story of Levi's

first pair of pants is entirely accurate. The San Francisco earthquake of 1906 destroyed many of the Levi Strauss & Co.'s records. What is certain, however, is that by the 1860s, men everywhere were wearing "those pants of Levi's."

Those Rivets

By 1866 Levi and David had expanded their partnership to include Levi's brothers, Louis and Jonas, and their brother-in-law, William Sahlein. William had married Levi's oldest sister, Mary. He worked with Levi and David in the San Francisco office, while Louis and Jonas supervised the manufacturing and importing of goods in New York. Although Levi was the youngest of the partners, he led the rest. He was respected for his keen business sense.

In that year, the partners in San Francisco purchased a warehouse at 14-16 Battery Street. The building that Levi and his partners chose was in the center of the rapidly developing business district. Nearby on the corner of Battery and Clay Streets was the three-story Merchants' Exchange Building. Here Levi could check on ship and cargo information, read foreign newspapers, and meet with other business leaders. Not far away, on Kearny Street, several retail shops were beginning to thrive. This small neighborhood was fast becoming the hub of dry-goods sales.

The partners remodeled and expanded the warehouse on Battery Street, adding gaslight chandeliers, a cast-iron front, and a newly patented freight elevator. The elevator, which may have been the only one of its kind in the city, was described in detail in an article about the company in the *San Francisco Chronicle*. "It works by hydraulic power . . . [and] carries a weight of 2,000 pounds. Accident is impossible. . . . The whole apparatus is handsomely ornamented." The elevator was the best and newest of its kind, demonstrating the great care Levi and his company put into the construction of their headquarters.

When the building was finally finished, Levi watched as workers hung the new company sign above the red stone columns.

"Levi Strauss & Co."

It looked good. Levi and his partners would rather have called the company, "Strauss Brothers," but that name had already been taken.

In its thirteen years, the business had accomplished a great deal. Many other dry goods establishments in the city had gone bankrupt. But the company of David Stern and Levi Strauss had survived and expanded.

The next two years, though, were not easy. In 1867 Levi's sister Mary died, leaving her husband, William, their daughter, and two sons.

In 1868 an earthquake shook San Francisco. This was the most severe earthquake the young city had yet experienced. Three years earlier, a smaller quake had shaken several buildings off their pilings. But the disaster of 1868 was the first San Francisco earthquake in which people were killed. Twelve people died in the terror and wreckage. Property damage was estimated at over $400,000. The enormous tremors cracked the structure of the new Levi Strauss & Co. building from top to bottom.

When the terrible shaking stopped, Levi hurried to check on his employees. All were slightly atremble but safe. The cracks in the building were repaired as quickly as possible, and business soon went on as it had before the earthquake.

By February 1872, the *Chronicle* noted with admiration the speed of the company's delivery service: "As soon as goods are ordered a large force of men immediately fill the bills. Whether goods are to be shipped or delivered in the city, the firm has their own teams to deliver the purchases made to their destination without a loss of time."

Levi Strauss & Co. was now selling dry goods and waist-high overalls far beyond California's borders to Oregon, Washington Territory, Vancouver Island, British Columbia, Alaska, Arizona, Nevada, Utah, Idaho, and the Hawaiian Islands.

Levi no longer went out peddling the company's goods. He employed ten salesmen to travel in his place. The young salesmen did not have to walk from town to town, as Levi had done. Instead, they traveled by train or ship, and on rare occasions by wagon—all at company expense. They toted catalogs and sample trunks instead of one-hundred-pound packs of merchandise. When they reached their destinations, they slept in hotels instead of alongside the road or in a farmer's barn.

But the salesmen were getting the job done. Sales rose with each passing year. Throughout the West, Levi Strauss & Co. was known as the only store of its kind to sell both clothing and dry goods on a wholesale basis. Store owners could easily purchase all the items they needed in one order or one stop. Even San Francisco shopkeepers bought from the company because its prices were cheaper than those of New York companies. In addition the city merchants did not have to worry about the dangers and delays of shipping when they bought goods from Levi Strauss & Co.

Across the country, Levi's name was held in high regard. The four-story building on Battery Street was a showcase for American and imported clothing, linens, and numerous household articles. The clothing department stocked mainly men's and boy's denim pants, shirts, and jackets. These items, according to the *Chronicle,* were "made to order by the leading New York firm of J. Strauss Bros. & Co." The foreign dry goods department carried "a very full assortment of English, German, and French hosiery, dress goods of every description for ladies and children, a complete variety of white goods, a full line of toilet quilts, Irish linens, table linens, towels, etc."

People who worked for Levi knew that they were expected to work as hard as he did and give their customers the best and quickest service they could.

The *Chronicle* was impressed by the tight ship Levi ran: "The large force of men engaged—salesmen, bookkeepers, clerks, assistants, porters, and teamsters—are always busy as bees." The store was open six days a week, from six o'clock in the morning until six o'clock at night. For many years, this is where Levi spent most of his time.

Every morning at nine o'clock, Levi left the Stern house at 317 Powell Street and walked the eight blocks to Battery Street. He was a striking figure in his shiny silk stovepipe hat and black split-tail coat.

As he strolled to work, Levi would stop and chat with neighboring shopkeepers. Some of them were his competitors, but they were also his friends.

Entering the store, Levi greeted his employees by name, and they replied, using his first name. For Levi, "Mr. Strauss" sounded too formal. He wanted his employees to feel a part of the family business. He took time to get acquainted with even the newest salesclerks. Hardworking employees were sure to get promoted.

Reaching his private office at the rear of the store, Levi set to work reviewing business transactions and proposals. From his office, he could see the entire wholesale clothing department.

If Levi spied a familiar customer, he would walk out to the floor for a visit. He knew from his peddler's days that business goes better with a friend than with a stranger.

Levi's days went by with a mixture of business decisions and meetings. At the end of each day, he checked sales figures with his trusted bookkeeper, Philip Fisher. Then it would be back home to the house at Powell Street.

Finally, as the sun set, Levi would once more put on his tophat and take a brisk walk to the St. Francis Hotel. An elegant table, a few close friends, and a sumptuous meal awaited him there.

Levi felt comfortable with his daily routine and the steadiness of his business. But one July morning in 1872, Levi received a letter that would change the company forever. It was from a customer named Jacob Davis, and it was addressed to the "Gents" of Levi Strauss & Co.

As a tailor in Reno, Nevada, Jacob Davis had been purchasing off-white duck cloth from Levi Strauss & Co. to make tents, horse blankets, and wagon covers. His most recent order, however, had been for some nine-ounce blue denim. He was not writing to complain about the cloth but to share a discovery he had made.

In December of 1870, a woman had come to Davis's shop asking him to make a pair of strong pants for her husband. The woman's husband was a large man who was constantly ripping the pocket seams of his pants. So Davis had made the new pair of pants. Just as the tailor was finishing them, he noticed some copper rivets lying on the counter. Davis thought he would try fastening the pant's pocket seams with rivets to make them more secure.

This was the answer. No matter how rugged the wear, the rivets kept the pockets from tearing. Since this time, Davis wrote, he had been swamped with requests for the riveted pants. "The secratt of them pents," the letter said, " is the Rivits that I put in those Pockets, and I found the demand so large that I cannot make them up fast enough."

At last count, Davis had made and sold nearly two hundred pairs of pants. He sent two pairs of riveted pants along with his letter so the company gents could see the tailor's discovery for themselves.

Davis's idea impressed Levi and his partners. The company made a deal with Davis, and together they applied for a patent on pants strengthened at all points of strain with copper rivets. A patent would protect the idea as their property. Then no one else could manufacture pants of the same kind in the United States.

Their patent application, however, was refused. The United States Patent Office said that similar rivets had been used on boots made for northern troops during the Civil War.

Levi and Jacob made changes in their application and tried again. And again. And again. Ten months later, on May 20, 1873, a patent was finally granted to Jacob Davis and Levi Strauss & Co. for their sturdy pants with copper rivets.

Even before the patent was granted, however, Jacob closed up shop in Reno and moved his wife, Annie, and their six children to San Francisco. Davis became the company's first production foreman, supervising the manufacturing of the riveted pants. He saw to it that the cloth was properly cut, bundled, and delivered every morning to the homes of seamstresses around San Francisco. Every evening Davis collected as many as five pairs of pants from each worker. The pants were made of off-white or brown canvas, or blue denim. Davis checked each pair carefully.

The riveted pants were a hit! The copper rivets made Levi's work pants even longer lasting.

Within several weeks, the demand for Levi's new pants grew so great that the partners decided to set up a manufacturing plant in San Francisco. This was a new venture for the company. Before the riveted pants, all the clothing for Levi Strauss & Co., including Levi's pants, had been made in New York by J. Strauss Brothers & Co.

After buying Davis's half share in the pants patent, Levi Strauss & Co. purchased the Donahue Building on Fremont Street. The company hired sixty women, each of whom would make five or six garments a day. For this amount of work, the seamstresses earned three dollars. And the more garments they finished, the more they earned. These women could go home proudly with as much money in their pockets as men who were doing hard labor.

Some of the women made blanket-lined pants and hunting jackets. Others sewed the riveted pants. These riveted denim pants were the original 501® jeans. The 501 indicated the lot number of the fabric. The pants were made from nine-ounce denim (later to become ten-ounce) and had tapered legs that could be easily tucked into the tops of boots. Each pair of jeans was slightly oversized. After washing, the pants would shrink to fit the wearer.

In 1873, the same year as the patent approval, Levi Strauss & Co. developed a trademark for its pants. It was a two-arc design that was stitched in orange thread on the jean's back pockets. The pattern looked like the wings of a seagull in flight. Jacob had chosen the orange thread to match the copper rivets.

Another trademark was in 1886—a leather patch sewn on the waistband of each pair of jeans. Branded on the patch was a picture of two horses trying to tear apart a pair of Levi's sturdy pants. This patch was a guarantee that these waist-high overalls could withstand the roughest wear possible. And, of course, the patch was attached to the pants with orange thread.

Although Levi did not live to see it, another trademark was added to his pants in 1936. This was the famous red-and-white tab that said "Levi's." It was attached to the seam of the right-hand back pocket of the 501® jeans.

All three of these trademarks—the two-arc design, the leather patch, and the red-and-white tab—are still being used by Levi Strauss & Co.

6

A Generous Hand

The year 1874 held good news and bad news for Levi Strauss & Co. The good news was that the company sold 5,875 dozen riveted pants, vests, coats, and shirts for $148,471. The bad news was that Levi lost his first partner, Fanny's husband, David Stern. David Stern died at the age of fifty-one. His eldest son, Jacob, a quiet and solemn young man, took his father's place in the business.

Levi was now forty-five years old and had never married. Fanny insisted that he continue to live with her and her seven children.

Later, when Fanny married her widowed brother-in-law, William Sahlein, Levi moved with them to a new home. Fortunately the house at the corner of Post and Leavenworth Streets was large enough to hold the thirteen members of the two families. Sometimes it even had to house Jonas Strauss's son, Nathan, who often visited from New York.

Levi taught all of his nephews much about how to run a company. He showed them how to build solid, friendly business relationships and how to seize opportunities when they come along.

In 1875 Levi saw one such opportunity arise. The Mission and Pacific Woolen Mills, which had long provided the company with woolen blankets and yard goods, was up for sale. Levi knew that over time the purchase of the mills would pay off. So without much hesitation, Levi Strauss & Co. bought the millworks.

In 1876 Levi made another bold move. With sales nearing $200,000, Levi sent Jacob Davis to New York City to open another manufacturing plant for the riveted denim pants. But Levi made sure the headquarters of the company remained where they had started—in San Francisco.

During the late 1800s, Levi made many large private purchases as well. His reputation as an important and respected leader in the San Francisco community grew. Several organizations, including the San Francisco Gas Company, asked him to be on their board of directors.

As a charter member and treasurer of the San Francisco Board of Trade, Levi was also active in urging the United States Congress to build a Central American canal. Levi remembered the long journey he had made around Cape Horn. He understood how much a ship's canal through Central America could speed up trade between New York and San Francisco.

No matter how busy Levi became, however, he always gave generously of his time and money to community organizations, often doing so anonymously. Levi took a special interest in helping young people, perhaps because he had never had children of his own. His Jewish heritage had taught him to care for the poor—non-Jew as well as Jew —and to give special consideration to widows and orphans. He gave large contributions to Jewish, Catholic, and Protestant orphanages.

Levi had never received much of a formal education. But he wanted hardworking students to have a chance for an education even if they didn't have much money. He provided Jewish students with scholarships to Hebrew school, and he established twenty-eight scholarships at the University of California—four scholarships for each of the seven Congressional districts.

In addition Levi served on the Board of Directors of the California School for the Deaf.

Over the years, he developed a special fondness for the school and its students. Along with large donations of time and money to the school, Levi also gave the school, oddly enough, a large bronze bell to hang in the clock tower of the campus.

From 1880 to 1890, Levi Strauss & Co. continued to prosper. The number of workers manufacturing Levi's clothing grew from 250 to 450. Levi may not have known all of their names, but they knew his. By this time, most people in the country knew Levi's name.

In 1890, when Levi was sixty-one, he made Fanny's sons—Jacob, Sigmund, Louis, and Abraham—partners in the firm. Although Levi now spent much of his time meeting with various boards and charitable committees, he remained the head of the company.

Levi never really retired from his business. His work had become his life. At the age of sixty-six, Levi told a reporter for the *San Francisco Bulletin,* "I've been in the harness for forty-three years, and I could not live without my daily duties. I am a bachelor, and I fancy on that account I need to work more, for my entire life is in my business. I don't believe that a man who once forms the habit of being busy can retire and be contented."

Even though he was a multimillionaire, Levi did not believe money was the key to happiness. He told the reporter for the *Bulletin,* "I do not think large fortunes cause happiness to their owners, for immediately those who possess them become slaves to their wealth. They must devote their lives to caring for their possessions. I don't think money brings friends to its owner. In fact, often the result is quite the contrary."

On September 26, 1902, Levi Strauss died in his sleep at the age of seventy-three. Nearly all the store owners in San Francisco closed their doors to attend the funeral services. Levi was a man they had trusted and admired. Several close friends and long-time employees acted as pallbearers at his funeral, and his body was buried in the Home of Peace Cemetery, north of San Francisco.

Levi Strauss & Co. was left in the capable hands of the four Stern brothers. Simon Davis, the son of the tailor Jacob Davis, followed his father as production supervisor. For several generations, the company was passed down through the families.

Over the decades following Levi's death, "those pants of Levi's" changed only slightly. During the early 1900s, complaints came to Levi Strauss & Co. that the jeans's back-pocket rivets were scratching saddles and school desks. The rivets were first covered with fabric and later removed.

Another suggestion for change came from some cowboys, as well as from Walter Haas, Sr. (the company's president from 1928 to 1955). Mr. Haas had been on a camping trip wearing, of course, Levi's jeans. He sat too near a campfire, and the rivets on the jeans became heated. Upon his return, Mr. Haas recommended to the Board of Directors that the rivet at the bottom of the zipper be removed. They agreed.

Some things have changed, but others have not. The family-owned company now makes a full line of clothing for men, women, and children, sold in over seventy countries. But the company is still best known for its sturdy denim pants—the 501® jeans.

Though Levi Strauss will always be remembered for the name he gave to a simple pair of pants, he must also be recognized for his charity and goodwill. According to his obituary in the *San Francisco Bulletin,* "Mr. Strauss was rated several times a millionaire, and he gave his wealth with a generous hand."

Levi cared about the world in which he lived, and in return the world will long remember him.

Sources

Boroff, David. "Little Milk, Little Honey," *American Heritage,* October, 1966, pp. 12+.

Cray, Ed. *Levi's.* Boston: Houghton Mifflin, 1978.

"Interview with Levi Strauss," *San Francisco Bulletin,* October 12, 1895, pp. 13-14.

Josephy, Alvin M. "Those Pants that Levi Gave Us," *American West,* July/August, 1985, pp. 30-37.

Kramer, William M. and Norton B. Stern. "Levi Strauss: The Man Behind the Myth," *Western States Jewish History,* April, 1987.

Lewis, Oscar. *Sea Routes to the Gold Fields.* New York: Knopf, 1949.

Meltzer, Milton. *The Jews in America.* Philadelphia: The Jewish Publication Society, 1985.

"Our Solid Merchants: The Immense Establishment of Levi Strauss & Co." *San Francisco Chronicle,* February 11, 1872.

Robbins, Peggy. "Levi Strauss," *American History Illustrated,* August, 1971, pp. 33-35.

Roth, Art. "The Levi's Story," *American Heritage,* Fall, 1952, pp. 49-51

Rupp, Becky. "In Praise of Bluejeans; the Denimization of America," *Blair Ketchum's Country Journal,* December, 1985, pp. 82-86.

Scull, Penrose. "Pack-Road to Yesterday," *American Heritage,* April, 1956, pp. 58-61.

Additional acknowledgements and gratitude go to the following people and organizations: Douglas Goldman, Mrs. Richard Goldman, and Mrs. Theodore Geballe (all relatives of Levi Strauss); Joyce Bustinduy, Dean Christon, Peggy Jue, and Lynn Downey of Levi Strauss & Co.; Harriet Nathan of the Bancroft Library, University of California; the California Historical Society; the California State Library at Sacramento; the American Museum of Immigration at Ellis Island; and the New York City Historical Society.